DISCOVERING AFRICA

EAST
AFRICA

Countries of East Africa

Burundi, Comoros and Mayotte, Djibouti, Eritrea, Ethiopia, Kenya, Madagascar, Mauritius, Réunion, Rwanda, Seychelles, Somalia, Tanzania, Uganda.

DISCOVERING AFRICA

EAST
AFRICA

Annelise Hobbs

MASON CREST

Mason Crest
450 Parkway Drive, Suite D
Broomall, PA 19008
www.masoncrest.com

Cataloging-in-Publication Data on file with the Library of
Congress.

Printed and bound in the United States of America.

First printing
9 8 7 6 5 4 3 2 1

ISBN: 978-1-4222-3717-5
Series ISBN: 978-1-4222-3715-1
ebook ISBN: 978-1-4222-8068-3
ebook series ISBN: 978-1-4222-8066-9

Produced by Regency House Publishing Limited
The Manor House
High Street
Buntingford
Hertfordshire
SG9 9AB
United Kingdom

www.regencyhousepublishing.com

Text copyright © 2017 Regency House Publishing
Limited/Annelise Hobbs

CONTENTS

KEY ICONS TO LOOK FOR:

 Words to Understand: These words with their easy-to-understand definitions will increase the reader's understanding of the text, while building vocabulary skills.

 Sidebars: This boxed material within the main text allows readers to build knowledge, gain insights, explore possibilities, and broaden their perspectives by weaving together additional information to provide realistic and holistic perspectives.

 Text-Dependent Questions: These questions send the reader back to the text for more careful attention to the evidence presented there.

Granite rock formations on the beautiful island of La Digue in the Seychelles.

BURUNDI

Burundi lies between DR Congo and Lake Tanganyika (Tanzania); it also includes part of the Great Rift Valley. The terrain is hilly or mountainous, sloping to a high plateau in the east.

Inhabited by Bantu-speaking Hutu and Tutsi peoples, Burundi has long been divided by ancient rivalries. The area was part of German East Africa from the 1890s until the First World War, when it came under Belgian administration as Urundi. It became an independent **monarchy** in 1962 and a republic in 1966.

Multi-party elections in 1993 brought the Hutus to power for the first time, rather then the Tutsis, who had long been used to having the upper hand; this led to massacre and violence within a few months and the murder of the first democratically elected Hutu president in 1993. In 1996 the Tutsi army seized power but the ethnic cleansing continued, despite **sanctions** and international censure. Since then, around 200,000 Burundis have perished, while hundreds of thousands more have been displaced or have fled to neighboring countries. In 1998 Burundi troops briefly joined the conflict in DR Congo.

An internationally brokered power-sharing agreement between the Tutsi-dominated government and the Hutu rebels in 2003 paved the way for a process of transition, leading to an integrated defense force, the drafting of a new

Words to Understand

Cease-fire: An agreement to temporarily stop fighting a war with a view to reconciliation.

Monarchy: A form of government in which a country is ruled by a king or queen.

Sanctions: Actions that are taken to force a country to obey international laws.

LEFT: Sunset in Burundi with lush vegetation in the foreground.

OPPOSITE: A map of Burundi.

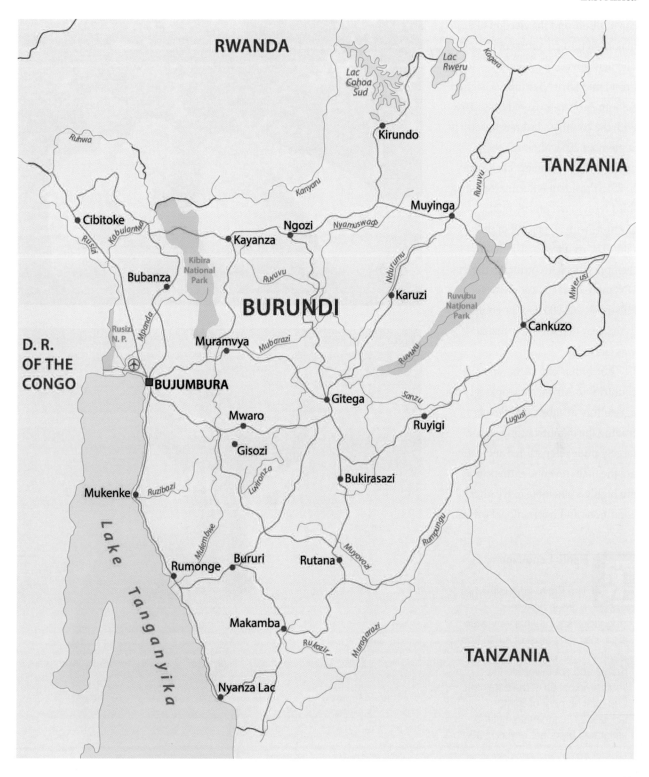

RWANDA

TANZANIA

Lac
Rweru

Lac
Cohoa
Sud

Kagera

Kirundo

Ruhwa

Kanyaru

Ruvuvu

Cibitoke

Muyinga

Kabulantwa

Ngozi

Nyamuswaga

Rusia

Kayanza

Nduruma

Mwerusi

Bubanza

Kibira
National
Park

Ruvuvu

Karuzi

Ruvubu
National
Park

Cankuzo

BURUNDI

Mpanda

Rusizi
N. P.

Muramvya

Mubarazi

Ruvuvu

D. R.
OF THE
CONGO

BUJUMBURA

Gitega

Sanzu

Lugusi

Mwaro

Ruyigi

Gisozi

Luhonza

Bukirasazi

Mukenke

Ruzibazi

Rumpungu

Mutembwe

Muyovozi

Lake Tanganyika

Rumonge

Bururi

Rutana

Muragarazi

Makamba

Rukazir-

TANZANIA

Nyanza Lac

constitution, and the election of a majority Hutu government in 2005. The new government, led by President Pierre Nkurunziza, signed a South African-brokered **cease-fire** with the country's last rebel group in September 2006, although the country still faces many challenges. In 2015 President Nkurunziza won a third term in the presidential elections with 70 percent of the vote. The result was disputed by the opposition. According to the UN, more than 400 people were killed and 260,000 fled the country in the year that Mr Nkurunziza was elected.

Burundi is one of the smallest countries in Africa. Its people rely on agriculture at subsistence level, leaving the manufacturing sector largely undeveloped. Tea and coffee are the main revenue earners, but are highly vulnerable to weather conditions and international prices.

Bantu Languages

The Bantu languages are a group of African languages spoken in a very wide area, including most of Africa from southern Cameroon, eastward to Kenya and southward to the southernmost tip of the continent. The total number of Bantu languages is uncertain, but it is estimated there are around 500.

OPPOSITE ABOVE: Breadfruit (*Artocarpus altilis*) is a species of flowering tree in the mulberry and jackfruit family. Originating in the South Pacific it can be found growing in many parts of Africa including Burundi.

OPPOSITE BELOW: The grey duiker (*Sylvicapra grimmia*) is found in large numbers in the eastern and southern savannas. It can be seen in the Ruvubu National Park, Burundi.

ABOVE: Lake Tanganyika is estimated to be the second largest freshwater lake in the world by volume.

Text-Dependent Questions

1. Which two peoples inhabit Burundi?

2. Who is the current president of Burundi?

3. Which two crops make the most revenue for Burundi?

COMOROS AND MAYOTTE

An archipelago of small volcanic islands in the Indian Ocean, lying north-west of Madagascar.

The Comoros were first visited by the British in the 16th century when Arab influence predominated. In the middle of the 19th century, the islands were under French

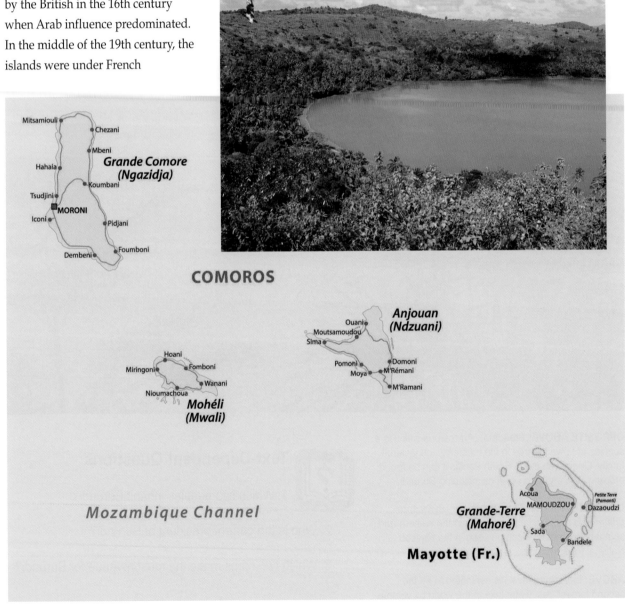

Grande Comore (Ngazidja)

Mitsamiouli • • Chezani
• Mbeni
Hahaia • • Koumbani
Tsudjini •
■ **MORONI**
Iconi •
• Pidjani
Dembeni • • Foumboni

COMOROS

Anjouan (Ndzuani)
Ouani •
Moutsamoudou •
Sima •
Pomoni • • Domoni
Moya • • M'Rémani
• M'Ramani

Mohéli (Mwali)
Hoani •
Miringoni • • Fomboni
• Wanani
Nioumachoua •

Mozambique Channel

Grande-Terre (Mahoré)
Acoua •
MAMOUDZOU ■
Petite Terre (Pamanti)
• Dazaoudzi
Sada •
• Bandele

Mayotte (Fr.)

Words to Understand

Copra: Dried white coconut flesh from which coconut oil is made.

Sisal: A fiber made from a tropical plant. It is widely used for cordage and making ropes.

Referendum: A public vote on a particular issue.

OPPOSITE ABOVE: Crater lake of Dziani, Mayotte.

ABOVE: The island of Anjouan.

protection, until Grande Comore (with the capital Moroni), Anjouan, and Mohéli chose independence in a referendum of 1974. In 1978, the Comoros, apart from Mayotte, which chose to remain united with France, became the Federal and Islamic Republic of the Comoros. Coconuts, **copra**, vanilla, **sisal**, and cocoa are the main products and exports of the islands.

Mayotte consists of the main island of Mahoré or Grande Terre, and the island of Pamanzi or Petite Terre. Its capital is Mamoudzou, on the island of Grande Terre. Mayotte is known as Mahoré by those who believe it should be included in the Republic of Comoros. In 2001 Mayotte's status changed to one approximating a département of mainland France. In 2009 the island

Text-Dependent Questions

1. Where is the archipelago of Comoros and Mayotte?

2. When was Comoros first visited by the British?

3. What is Mayotte's main source of income?

of Mayotte voted to become fully integrated with France. However, the Comoros government who has laid claim to the islands termed the **referendum** null and void.

Mayotte has an agricultural economy, producing bananas and mangos. The total area of Mayotte is 144 square miles (374km²), and the population numbers around 186,500.

Mont Choungui

Mont Choungui is a distinctively shaped, volcanic mountain in the south of Mayotte.

Its unusual shape dominates the southern peninsula of the island. The whole area is mainly forested with areas of shrubland and thickets where the baobab tree (*Adansonia digitata*) grows. The area has been identified as an important habitat for birds, particularly because it supports significant populations of Comoros olive pigeons (*Columba pollenii*), Comoros blue-pigeons (*Alectroenas sganzini*), Mayotte white-eyes (*Zosterops mayottensis*), Mayotte sunbirds (*Cinnyris coquerellii*), and red-headed fodies (*Foudia eminentissima*). The area is also home to various species of rare geckos and sea turtles.

DJIBOUTI

Djibouti is strategically linked by rail with Addis Ababa, and is Ethiopia's main outlet for overseas trade. Indeed, much of Djibouti's economy is based on this fact, as well as her status as a free trade zone in north-east Africa.

The country is a seductive mix of African, Indian, European, and Arab influences. Formerly French Somaliland from 1892–1967 and the French Territory of the Afars and the Issas (the two main ethnic groups) from 1967–77, the republic is situated in the Afro-Asian Rift Valley system on the Gulf of Tadjoura, where the Red Sea and the Gulf of Aden meet. Lake Assal, at 508 feet (155m) below sea level, is the lowest point in Africa. Much of the remainder of the country is an arid, unproductive plain, apart from the Mabla Mountains that back the

ABOVE: The dried out Lake Abbe, also known as Lake Abhe Bad, is a salt lake lying on the Ethiopia-Djibouti border.

OPPOSITE: A map of Djibouti.

Words to Understand

Balance of payments: A summary of international transactions over a period of time.

Civil war: A war between groups of people in the same country.

Sub-Saharan Africa: Relating to the part of Africa south of the Sahara desert.

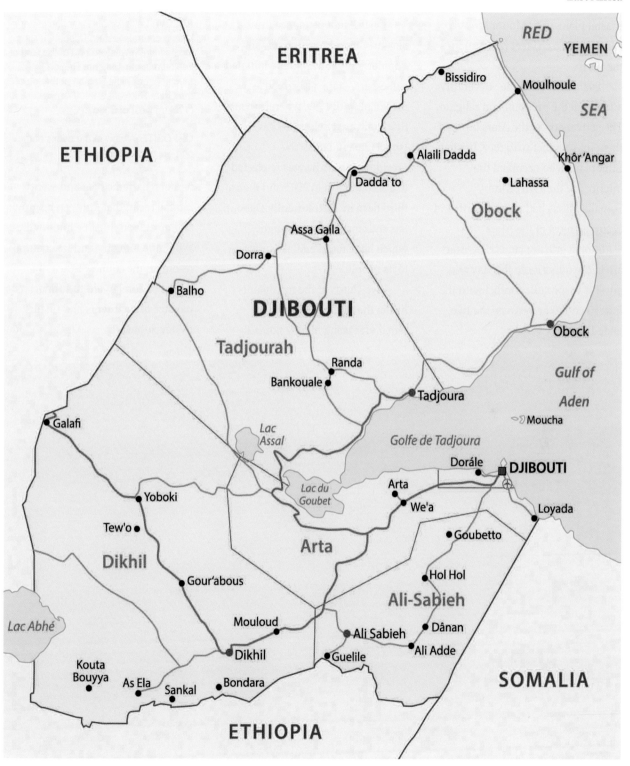

coastal plain, with Mount Moussa Ali rising to 6,653 feet (2,028m) in the north.

Islam arrived in the 9th century and is still the predominant religion. The conversion of the Afars brought them into conflict with the Christian Ethiopians who occupied the interior. By the 19th century, Somalian Issas had moved north and occupied most of the Afars' traditional grazing lands. The Afars are in the minority to this day and are still in sporadic conflict with the Issas; a **civil war** between the two ended in 2001.

On full independence in 1977, Hassan Gouled Aptidon, of the Popular Rally for Progress, initiated a one-party state. He served as president until 1999, when Djibouti's first multi-party elections gave Ismail Omar Guellah the presidential seat; he was re-elected to a second term in 2005 and then a third term in 2011. Recently Djibouti has endured years of drought which has caused endless suffering to its people.

Two-thirds of the inhabitants live in the capital, Djibouti, the remainder being mostly nomadic

BELOW: Lake Assal is a saline crater lake in central-western Djibouti. It is located at the western end of the Gulf of Tadjoura in the Tadjoura Region, touching the Dikhil Region at the top of the Great Rift Valley. It is 74 miles (120km) west of Djibouti City.

OPPOSITE: A view of the docks at the port of Djibouti.

herders. Extreme heat and scanty rainfall mean that little can be grown and most food must be imported. With little industry and few natural resources the country is heavily reliant on foreign aid to support its **balance of payments** and finance its development.

Djibouti continues to have political ties with Somaliland, though most of the 26,000 Somalis, who sought refuge during the civil unrest of the 1990s, have since returned home.

France maintains a military presence in Djibouti, which currently hosts the only US military base in **sub-Saharan Africa**; this is a useful tool in the current fight against terrorism. In May, 2014 a bomb exploded in a restaurant killing three, including two suicide bombers. The Somali Islamist group al-Shabab claimed responsibility.

Text-Dependent Questions

1. Which countries have influenced Djibouti's culture?

2. In what century did the religion of Islam arrive?

3. When was full independence achieved?

ERITREA

An independent state in north-east Africa, Eritrea is bordered by Ethiopia, Djibouti, and Sudan, and has a strategically important 715-mile (1150-km) coastline on the Red Sea. There is a hot, dry, desert strip along the Red Sea coast, with an area of highland in the center and north-west (a continuation of the high Ethiopian plateau), while flat to rolling semi-arid plains cover the south-west. There are frequent droughts, but irrigation allows a few crops to be grown.

Eritrea was under Egyptian rule in earlier times, when it was described as the legendary Land of Punt. It was a dependency of Ethiopia until the 16th century, when it fell to the Ottoman empire. From 1890 to 1941 Eritrea was an

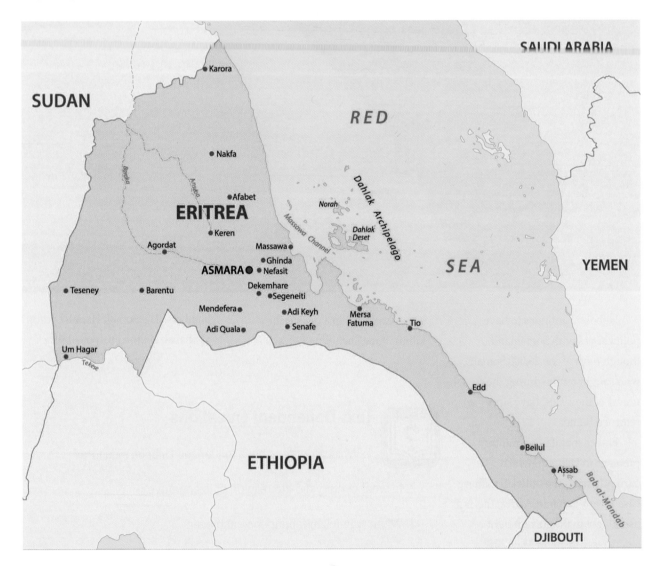

OPPOSITE: A map of Eritrea.

BELOW: Asmara is the capital city and largest settlement in Eritrea.

Words to Understand

Guerrilla: A member of a small group of soldiers who do not belong to a regular army and who fight independently.

Refugees: People who have been forced to leave a country for religious, war, or political reasons.

Unicameral: A government consisting of a single legislative assembly.

Debub Region
The high plateau in the southern region of Eritrea is the location of the ancient city of Qohaito, an ancient center of the Aksumite kingdom.

Ancient rock art (pictured right) near Qohaito in the Adi Alauti Cave suggest habitation in the area since the fifth millennium BC.

The Debub region is the location of Eritrea's highest mountain, Mount Emba Soira, rising to 9,902 feet (3,018m).

ABOVE: Sheikh Hanafi Mosque stands on the Piazza degli Incendi in the center of the old city of Massawa. The mosque dates back to the 15th century and is one of the oldest surviving buildings in the city.

Massawa or Mitsiwa is a port city on the Red Sea coast of Eritrea located at the northern end of the Gulf of Zula beside the Dahlak Archipelago. Massawa is one of the world's hottest places, with an annual average temperature of 86°F (30ºC). Massawa is significant tourist area with notable architecture demonstrating Arab and Italian influences.

Italian colony, created from Ottoman territory and coastal areas of Ethiopia. In 1935 Italy used Eritrea as a base from which to pursue its conquest of Ethiopia, which became part of Italian East Africa in 1936. In 1941 Eritrea was made a protectorate of Britain, following Italy's removal from East Africa. After this, it was taken into British administration until 1952, and was made an autonomous region in federation with Ethiopia. In 1962 it was annexed by Ethiopia and was harshly subjugated. Ethiopia was particularly loath to relinquish its hold on Eritrea, being reliant on the Eritrean ports of Aseb and Massawa, the latter one of the largest ports in East Africa, as its only outlets to the sea.

A 30-year struggle for independence ensued, fought as **guerrilla** warfare by the Eritrean

25

Text-Dependent Questions

1. Which three countries border Eritrea?

2. What was Eritrea described as under Egyptian rule?

3. Why is agriculture so challenging in Eritrea?

People's Liberation Front (EPLF); during this time 150,000 were killed and 700,000 refugees fled to Sudan. By 1978 the EPLF had succeeded in driving all Ethiopian forces from Eritrean territory, but the situation was reversed when the Soviets intervened, backing Colonel Mengistu's Marxist regime. There was severe famine in Eritrea in the 1980s, followed by a refugee crisis due to Ethiopia's policy of forcible resettlement.

After the fall of Mengistu's Ethiopian government in 1991, Eritrea became internally self-governing. It became fully independent in May 1993, when thousands of Eritrean **refugees** began to return home.

In 1998 a border dispute between Eritrea and Ethiopia erupted, with bombing by both sides, which soon escalated into war. War ended in 2000 after the intervention of the UN; since then, a security zone on the border has been monitored by a UN peace-keeping operation. Despite an international commission in 2002, designed to settle the dispute once and for all, the matter remains to be fully resolved. Head of state and leader of the EPLF government since independence in 1993 is President Isaias Afwerki, who presides over a **unicameral** National Assembly of 150 seats.

Since independence, Eritrea, a desperately poor country, has had many problems to face, especially in the aftermath of the Ethiopian-Eritrean War of 1998–2000, when property, livestock, and homes were destroyed and the planting of crops was prevented. Most of the population relies on agriculture at subsistence level, but is constantly at the mercy of erratic rainfall.

Eritrea's economic future is also dependent on overcoming its many social problems, which include illiteracy, poor levels of skills, and unemployment. In 2015 a UN report accused the government of Eritrea of carrying out systematic, widespread, and gross human rights violations. The government dismissed this report as being politically motivated.

LEFT: Located in the Red Sea near the city port of Massawa, the Dahlak archipelago is an island group consisting of two large and 124 small islands. The pearl fisheries of the archipelago have been famous since Roman times and still produce a substantial number of pearls. Only four of the islands are permanently inhabited, of which Dahlak Kebir is the largest and most populated.

ETHIOPIA

Geographically, Ethiopia's most dominant feature is the massive range of volcanic mountains that rise at Ras Dashen in the north to over 15,000 feet (4575m). Ethiopia is divided by the Great Rift Valley into the Eastern and Western Highlands, the latter being the source of the Blue Nile. To the northeast is the Denakil Desert, forming Ethiopia's border with Eritrea, while the Ogaden Desert lies to the

Words to Understand

Coptic Christianity: Christianity originating in Egypt.

Marxist: A person who adheres to the theories of Karl Marx.

Multi-party system: A government where two or more political parties run for election.

south-east and borders Somalia.

Ethiopia (previously Abyssinia) has a longer history than any other African country, in that it dates from the 2nd millennium BC. According to legend, it was founded in around

OPPOSITE: Addis Ababa is the capital and largest city in Ethiopia.

BELOW: A map of Ethiopia.

1000 BC by Menelik I, son of King Solomon and the Queen of Sheba. Ethiopia is also claimed to be the final resting place of the Ark of the Covenant, once kept in the Temple of Solomon in Jerusalem, which held the tablets of the law given by God to Moses, and which was carried by the Israelites during their wanderings in the wilderness.

Situated in Tigray, in northern Ethiopia, is Axum (Aksum), once the capital of a powerful ancient kingdom, even though it later

fragmented. It was here that **Coptic Christianity**, introduced from Egypt in the 4th century and still the predominant religion, flourished. The Arab conquests of the 7th century isolated Axum from the rest of Christendom. Today, the dominant Amhara and related peoples are of mixed Hamitic and Semitic origins and are Coptic Christians, while the second largest group, the Muslims, are chiefly centered in Harar. There is a Jewish minority, the Falashas, living in the area north of Lake Tana, 10,000 of whom, during the famine of 1984–85, were airlifted to Israel.

Contact with Europe was established in the 16th century by the Portuguese and was renewed when the Scottish explorer, James Bruce, found the source of the Blue Nile in 1770. In the late 19th century, Menelik II (1889–1913) expanded the

BELOW: One of Ethiopia's favorite tourist attractions, The Blue Nile Falls (or *Tis Issat*, meaning smoking river), are considered to be one of the greatest falls in Africa. The misty deluge produces a shimmering effect across the gorge and often rainbows. The area is also a haven for tropical birds and monkeys.

empire and established Addis Ababa as his capital. Between 1897 and 1908, Abyssinia was a colonial power, encompassing Somali and

The Church of St. George, Lalibela

Dating back to the late 12th or early 13th century, the Church of St. George was constructed during the reign of King Gebre Mesquel Lalibela of the late Zagwe dynasty. The church was carved from a single limestone rock. Lalibela is a pilgrimage site for members of the Ethiopian Orthodox Tewahedo Church. There is a belief that pilgrims share the same blessing as pilgrims to Jerusalem. The site is part of the UNESCO World Heritage Site "Rock-Hewn Churches, Lalibela."

other peoples within its feudal empire. In 1930, Menelik's son, Ras Tafari, became emperor as Haile Selassie I (the "Lion of Judah"), but was deposed and exiled in Britain when Italy occupied Ethiopia in 1936–41, combining the country with Eritrea and Somalia to form Italian East Africa. Haile Selassie was restored to power by the British, during the Second World War, when the Italians were ejected, and he continued to rule until he was overthrown by a **Marxist** military junta in 1974, when a one-party state was established.

The 1960s were characterized by violent conflict with Eritrea, which had been federated with Ethiopia since 1952 but now demanded independence. Ethiopia responded by annexing Eritrea in 1962. By the 1970s the region's droughts and famines had taken their toll and

Haile Selassie began to lose popular support. He was deposed by Colonel Mengistu Haile Mariam in a military coup in 1974 and died while under arrest. (Haile Selassie continues to be revered by the Rastafarians, a sect that regards him as their messiah.)

In 1976 Mengistu initiated a reign of terror in which thousands of people died. He then proceeded to recapture territories in Eritrea and the Ogaden with Soviet assistance. There was widespread famine in 1984–85. In 1991, a coalition of rebel forces, the EPRDF (Ethiopian People's Revolutionary Democratic Front) and the EPLF (Eritrean People's Liberation Front) overthrew Mengistu, while 1995 saw the creation of the Federal Democratic Republic of Ethiopia. Girma Woldegiorgis was elected president and Meles Zenawi became prime minister of a **multi-party system** of government. In 1999, more than 40,000 people perished in a border war with Eritrea. The war ended in December 2000, though demarcation is still being disputed. Tension between Eritrea and and Ethiopia continues today.

One of the world's most impoverished countries, the population survives on subsistence

ABOVE: The Fasilides Castle in Gondar was the stronghold of Fasilides who was emperor of Ethiopia from 1632–1667. He was a member of the Solomonic dynasty. The castle is a UNESCO World Heritage Site.

OPPOSITE: The Dallol volcanic crater or hydrothermal field is located in the Danakil Depression in north-east Ethiopia. The vast Dallol landscape is truly spectacular and is said to be the hottest place on Earth. It is famous for its mulicolored salt, sulphur, and other mineral deposits that crystallize to form bizarre structures. At 157 feet (48m) below sea level, Dallol is Earth's lowest land volcano.

agriculture which is frequently affected by severe drought. Coffee is critical to the economy and Ethiopia remains heavily dependent on foreign food subsidies and financial aid from abroad.

Text-Dependent Questions

1. What was Ethiopia's former name?

2. What neighboring country to Ethiopia borders the Ogaden desert?

3. What decade saw widespread famine in Ethiopia?

KENYA

Mount Kenya gave its name to the country and at 17,058 feet (5199m) is the second highest mountain in Africa. The Republic of Kenya straddles the equator and has land borders with Uganda, Sudan, Ethiopia, Somalia, and Tanzania. From the tropical coastal plain, bordering the Indian Ocean, the land rises to more temperate highlands in

Words to Understand

Corruption: Illegal or dishonest behavior, particularly by those in power.

Miocene period: Relating to an epoch of the Tertiary Period, occurring from 25 to 10 millon years ago.

Plantations: Farms or estates in tropical or subtropical locations.

the west that are crossed by the Great Rift Valley.

The British Kenyan-born archeologist, Louis Leakey (1903–72), discovered gigantic animal fossils at the Olduvai Gorge in 1958, his wife, Mary, having previously found the skull of an ape-man of the **Miocene period** on Rusinga Island in Lake Victoria in 1948. In 1972, their son, Richard, discovered the earliest human bones ever found near the shores of Lake Turkana (Rudolf) in the

LEFT: Mount Kenya is one of the most impressive landscapes in East Africa. It is the highest mountain in Kenya and the second-highest in Africa, after Kilimanjaro. It is an ancient extinct volcano. The highest peak is Batian at 17,057 feet (5,199m).

OPPOSITE: A map of Kenya.

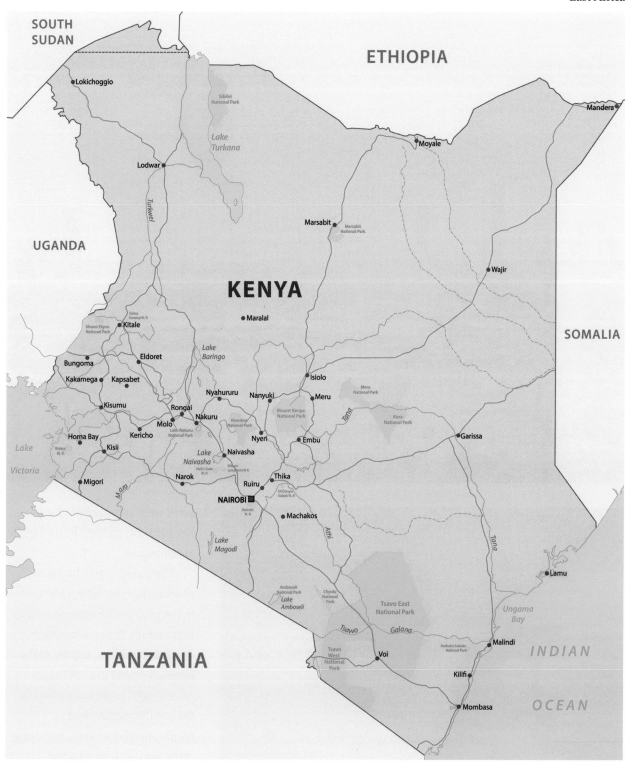

north-west; consequently, Kenya can justifiably claim to be the "cradle of civilization."

Populated largely by Bantu-speaking peoples, Kenya was settled by Arabs in the 8th century. In the 16th century, Portuguese traders dominated the area, but the Arabs regained control in 1729. Britain gained rights to the coastal area in the late 19th century and colonization began at the beginning of the next, on land acquired from the Kikuyu, on which **plantations** and farms were established. Kenya became a British crown colony in 1920.

The Mau Mau, a Kikuyan terrorist secret society, with nationalist aims, was active during the 1950s, focusing their attacks on European settlers in the south-western Kenyan Highlands. This resulted in a state of emergency being declared, the presence of British troops, and the imprisonment of Jomo Kenyatta for his alleged involvement with the Mau Mau. The conflict ended in 1960, by which time thousands had died, including even more Mau Mau. Kenyatta was released from prison in 1961, when he became president of the Kenya African National Union (KANU), which led Kenya to independence in 1963. A republic was established the following year, and Kenyatta became Kenya's first prime minister, becoming president the following year. Kenyatta's was an

OPPOSITE ABOVE: Nairobi, capital city of Kenya.

OPPOSITE BELOW: A safari game drive. Wildebeest (*Connochaetes gnou* and *C. taurinus*) and Mount Kilimanjaro are in the background.

ABOVE: The cheetah (*Acinonyx jubatus*), also known as the hunting leopard, is a big cat that occurs mainly in eastern and southern Africa.

Text-Dependent Questions

1. What is the second highest mountain in Africa?

2. What was the profession of Louis Leakey?

3. By which method of transport are vegetables grown in Kenya transported to Europe?

authoritarian rule, but he tried to establish unity, though drought and territorial disputes with Uganda and Tanzania caused civil unrest.

The years 1967–68 saw the departure of Asians from Kenya, many to Britain, following a period of intense Africanization. Kenya was a virtual one-party state from 1969–82, under the dominance of KANU. In 1978, Kenyatta died and

was succeeded as president by Daniel Arap Moi, who was re-elected in multi-party elections in 1992 and 1997. Moi created the first coalition government in 2001 and was succeeded by President Mwai Kibaki the following year, when he defeated the KANU candidate, Uhuru Kenyatta.

In 1998 the US embassy in Nairobi was bombed, killing nearly

ABOVE: African elephants (*Loxodonta africana*) in Amboseli National Park with Mount Kilimanjaro in the background.

OPPOSITE: Pink flamingos In Lake Nakuru.

250 people and injuring thousands more, while a terrorist car-bomb in a Mombasa hotel took more lives in 2002.

Kenya is still a developing country, but it is one of the most agriculturally productive in Africa, and tea, coffee, wheat, sugar, cotton, sisal, tobacco, rice, and timber are grown and dairy cattle and beef are raised. There is a luxury trade in flowers, fruit, and vegetables that are air-freighted to Europe, providing out-of-season produce when it is unavailable at home.

After some early progress in rooting out **corruption** and encouraging donor support, the Kibaki government was rocked by high-level corruption scandals in 2005 and 2006. In 2006 the World Bank and IMF delayed loans to Kenya pending action to quell corruption, and have since resumed lending, despite little action on the government's part to deal with the problem. Today, Kenya is a country with great ethnic diversity and a vibrant culture, however this has become a source of conflict. The

Islamist militant Al-Shabab movement has been launching a number of attacks in Kenya, including the 2013 Westgate shopping mall in Nairobi and the attack on Garissa University College in north-west Kenya. Other pressing challenges include high unemployment, crime, and poverty. Droughts frequently put millions of people at risk.

Kenya has an abundance of wildlife and many game reserves. Its beach resorts also attract thousands of tourists every year.

MADAGASCAR

The fourth-largest island in the world, Madagascar lies 240 miles (390km) off the south-east coast of Africa, separated from it by the Mozambique Channel. The narrow coastal plain rises to central highlands, while three great massifs lie in the north, the highest of which is the volcanic Tsaratanara, which peaks at 9,468 feet (2886m).

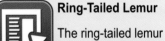

Words to Understand

Cash crop: A crop that is grown to be sold rather than for use by the farmer.

Deforestation: The act of clearing forests.

Martial law: Control of a country or area by military forces.

Ring-Tailed Lemur

The ring-tailed lemur (*Lemur catta*) is a primate and most recognized lemur due to its long, vividly-striped, black-and-white ringed tail. Like all lemurs it is only found on the island of Madagascar. The Lemur's diet is mainly fruit, but it also eat leaves, tree bark, flowers, and sap.

Ring-tailed lemurs live in troops of up to 30 individuals with a dominant female presiding over the group. To keep warm and reaffirm social bonds, groups will sit closely together. They will also sunbathe, preferring to show their underside, with its thinner white fur towards the sun. Ring-tailed lemurs are now classified as endangered, largely because the dry forests they inhabit are disappearing.

OPPOSITE: A map of Madagascar.

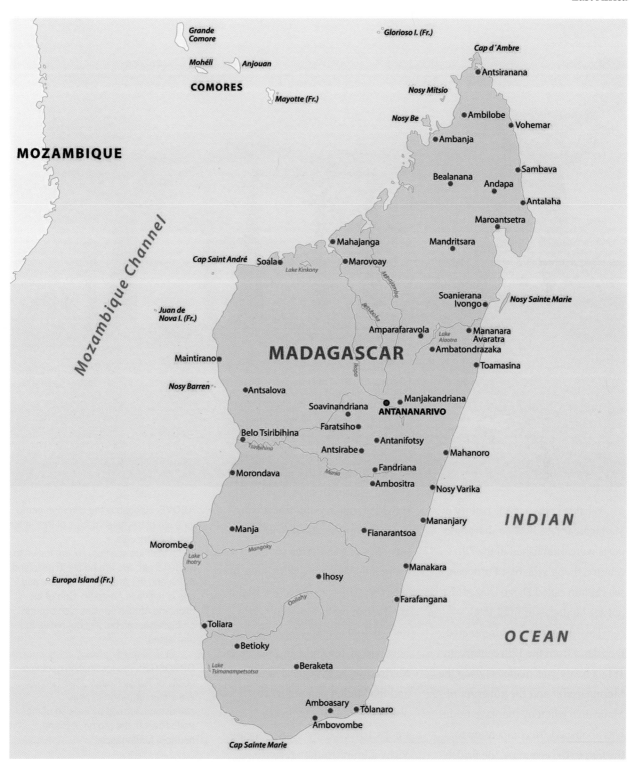

Grande Comore

Glorioso I. (Fr.)

Cap d´Ambre

Mohéli   Anjouan

Antsiranana

COMORES

Nosy Mitsio

Mayotte (Fr.)

Nosy Be   Ambilobe

Vohemar

Ambanja

MOZAMBIQUE

Sambava

Bealanana   Andapa

Antalaha

Maroantsetra

Mahajanga   Mandritsara

Cap Saint André   Soala   Marovoay

Lake Kinkony

Soanierana
Ivongo   Nosy Sainte Marie

Juan de
Nova I. (Fr.)

Amparafaravola   Mananara
Avaratra

MADAGASCAR   Lake
Alaotra   Ambatondrazaka

Maintirano   Toamasina

Nosy Barren

Antsalova

Soavinandriana   Manjakandriana
ANTANANARIVO

Faratsiho

Belo Tsiribihina   Antanifotsy

Tsiribihina   Antsirabe   Mahanoro

Fandriana

Morondava   Mania   Ambositra   Nosy Varika

Mananjary

Manja   Fianarantsoa

Morombe   Mangoky

Lake
Ihotry   Manakara

Europa Island (Fr.)   Ihosy

Farafangana

Onilahy

Toliara

Betioky

Lake
Tsimanampetsotsa   Beraketa

Amboasary   Tôlanaro

Ambovombe

Cap Sainte Marie

Mozambique Channel

Menarandra *Betsiboka* *Ikopa*

INDIAN

OCEAN

What is known of the history of Madagascar tells how Arab trading posts were established in the 7th century, though the first European, a sea captain called Diego Díaz, did not see Madagascar until 1500.

The Merina people dominated the island from the 17th century. In 1817 a treaty was made between the Merina leader and the governor of Mauritius, whereby the slave trade was abolished. To compensate for the loss to the economy, the British provided military and financial assistance to the island, with members of the Merina court eventually becoming Christians. In 1885 the British accepted the island as a French protectorate in return for eventual control of Zanzibar, now part of Tanzania. In 1895–96 the Merina fought the French and lost and the Merina monarchy was abolished. In 1942–43 British troops arrived to overthrow the pro-Vichy administration, restoring a

ABOVE: Baobab is the common name for each of the nine species of tree in the genus Adansonia.

Of the nine species, six are native to Madagascar, two are native to mainland Africa and the Arabian Peninsula, and one is native to Australia. One of the mainland African species also occurs on Madagascar, but it is not native to that island.

OPPOSITE: The fascinating geologic oddity of Tsingy Rouge (Red Tsingy) is a stone formation of pink standstone, formed by erosion of the Irodo River in the region of Diana, northern Madagascar.

Text-Dependent Questions

1. Who is Madagascar's current president?

2. How far is the island of Madagascar from mainland Africa?

3. What weather event hit Madagascar in 2000?

Free-French government to what was by now Malagasy. A national uprising was brutally suppressed by the French in 1947–48, when as many as 80,000 islanders are thought to have died.

Malagasy became a fully independent state within the French Community in 1960, with Philibert Tsiranana of the Social Democrat Party its first president. However, his autocratic rule proved unpopular, especially when he planned to link the economy with South Africa's apartheid regime. In 1972, a Merina-dominated military overthrew Tsiranana's government, and the economy took a sudden dive. **Martial law** was imposed in 1975, when Malagasy became Madagascar. A new one-party Marxist state was then adopted, with Lieutenant-Commander Didier Ratsiraka as president. However, he abandoned Marxism, which had involved nationalization and the severing of connections with France in 1980. A multi-party system of

ABOVE: Antananarivo is the capital and largest city in Madagascar.

OPPOSITE: The Anja Community Reserve was created in 2001 to help preserve the local environment and wildlife, but also to provide employment for the surrounding community. The reserve is mainly woodland and a freshwater lake, with boulders and fallen rocks strewn throughout. It also has two caves which provide an important habitat for wildlife. Tourists can use the trails accompanied by a local guide.

government became legal in 1990.

Following anti-government demonstrations, Ratsiraka established a government that included opposition members the following year. Constitutional reform was approved by referendum in 1992, and multi-party elections were held the following year. Ratsiraka was re-elected in 1997. In 1998 Tantely Andrianarivo was elected prime minister. In 2000, over half a million people were made homeless when cyclones hit the island, and political and ethnic violence followed the election in 2001. In 2002 Marc Ravalomanana became president when Ratsiraka fled the island following disputes with his rival, which averted civil war. Madagascar's current president is Hery Rajaonarimampianina who was sworn in following presidential elections in 2014.

From modest beginnings, Madagascar has achieved slow and steady growth since the middle of the 1990s. Agriculture, forestry, and fishing are the mainstays of the economy, though **deforestation** is a cause for concern. Coffee is a major **cash crop**. However, the unique diversity of Madagascar's flora and fauna may prove to be the making of the country, by attracting more and more ecotourists to its shores.

MAURITIUS

Lying in the Indian Ocean 500 miles (800km) or so east of Madagascar, the territory consists of the main island of Mauritius, almost entirely surrounded by **coral reefs**, the island of Rodrigues, 20 or so nearby islets, and the dependencies of the Agalega Islands; it also includes the tiny Cargados Carajos

Words to Understand

Coral reef: A line of coral that lies in warm and shallow water.

Human rights: Rights belonging to all people.

Philatelist: A person who collects and studies postage stamps.

shoals (Saint Brandon Rocks). The French island of Réunion lies 125 miles (200km) to the south-west.

Collectively, the archipelago is known as the Mascarene Islands; they were formed by undersea volcanic eruptions when the African plate drifted over the Réunion hotspot. However, they have long since ceased to be volcanically active.

The Portuguese discovered the then-uninhabited islands at the beginning of the 16th century, where they found a previously unknown bird, which they called the *doudo*

LEFT: Port Louis is the capital city of Mauritius and is also the country's cultural, economic, and political center. In use since 1638, the harbor is well-protected from strong winds by the Moka mountain range. It is the biggest harbor in Mauritius that supports thriving businesses. Port Louis is a vibrant and charming city, with interesting architecture both old and new.

RIGHT: A map of Mauritius.

(dodo) or simpleton, because it had no fear of man and could be easily killed. Sadly, the dodos had all disappeared by 1681, either killed by settlers or by their domestic animals.

The Dutch occupied the islands from 1598–1710, and named them Mauritius, after Prince Maurice of Nassau. Mauritius was controlled by the French from 1715 until the British took control in 1810, it being ceded to Britain in 1814. Mauritius was the fifth country in the world to issue postage stamps, the first of which, issued in 1847, are highly prized by

Le Morne Brabant

Le Morne Brabant is one of the most iconic sites in Mauritius. It is a peninsula at the extreme south-western tip on the windward side of the island. It is highlighted by an eponymous standing rock formation with a summit 1,824 feet (559m) above sea level. The peninsula is famous for its beaches, lagoons, plants, and wildlife. In the 19th century slaves were known to take shelter in caves on the mountainside. Le Morne Brabant has been a UNESCO World Heritage Site since 2008.

philatelists; they are extremely valuable because of their rarity.

In 1968 Mauritius achieved independence within the Commonwealth of Nations. More than half the people are Indo-Mauritians, descendants of laborers imported from India after the abolition of slavery in the 19th century, the remainder being of African, French, Chinese, or mixed descent.

Prime Minster and head of Government is Sir Anerood Jugnauth. The president is currently Ameenah Gurib-Fakim.

For most of the period since independence Mauritius has achieved an annual growth in the order of 5–6 percent. This has given it one of Africa's highest per capita incomes, while a stable democracy, regular free elections, and a positive human rights record, has attracted considerable investment from abroad.

Recent poor weather, declining sugar prices and textile and apparel production have tended to slow economic growth, leading to some protests over standards of living in the Creole community. Nevertheless, Mauritius has steadily-growing industrial, financial, and tourism sectors.

OPPOSITE:
The magnificent Waterfalls of Chamarel on the River St. Denis have a height of 272 feet (83m). A favorite for tourists, the site is famous for its wonderful views, lush vegetation, and gorges.

RIGHT: Also in Chamarel, is the natural phenomenon of the Seven Colored Earths. It is a small area of dinstinctively colored sand dunes that were formed by a combination of tropical weather and the geological conditions of the area.

Text-Dependent Questions

1. What nation discovered the then-uninhabited islands of Mauritius in the 16th century?

2. Why did the dodo become extinct so easily?

3. When did Mauritius gain independence?

RÉUNION

The largest of the Mascarene Islands, Réunion is a volcanically-active subtropical island in the Indian Ocean, east of Madagascar. It is rugged, mountainous, and forested in the interior, surrounded by a fertile coastal plain that is intensively cultivated. The highest point is the Piton des Neiges at 10,076 feet (3070m). Piton de la Fournaise, on the south-eastern coast, is still volcanically active, and devastating **cyclones** occur from time to time.

Words to Understand

Cyclone: A very destructive and powerful storm with high winds in a low pressure weather system.

Hydropower: Electricity generated from machines that are run by moving water.

Trade route: A route followed by traders.

Their progress in Réunion and the rest of the Indian Ocean is monitored from a station at Saint-Denis, the capital.

Discovered by the Portuguese in 1513, Réunion was annexed by Louis XIII of France in 1642, becoming part of France overseas in 1972. Until

OPPOSITE: Scenic view of Piton de la Fournaise volcano situated in the south-east corner of Réunion. It is one of the world's most active volcanoes,

BELOW: A map of Réunion.

1869, when the Suez Canal was opened, the island was important as a stopover on the **trade route** to the East Indies.

Head of state is the president of France, François Hollande, while Didier Robert is currently president of Réunion's regional council.

The white and Indian populations are far more prosperous than other segments of the population, and this causes social tensions, an example being the riots of 1991. The high unemployment that exists on the island is predominantly among the poor. It is

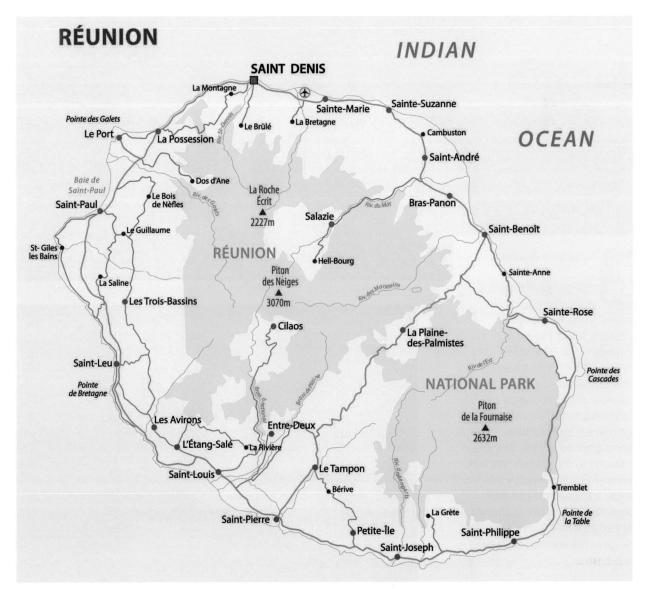

RÉUNION

SAINT DENIS

INDIAN

OCEAN

La Montagne
Pointe des Galets
Le Port
La Possession
Le Brûlé
La Bretagne
Sainte-Marie
Sainte-Suzanne
Cambuston
Saint-André
Riv. St-Denis
Baie de Saint-Paul
Dos d'Ane
Le Bois de Nèfles
Saint-Paul
La Roche Écrit ▲ 2227m
Riv. des Galets
Salazie
Riv. du Mât
Bras-Panon
Saint-Benoît
Le Guillaume
St-Giles les Bains
RÉUNION
Hell-Bourg
Sainte-Anne
La Saline
Piton des Neiges ▲ 3070m
Riv. des Marsouins
Les Trois-Bassins
Cilaos
La Plaine-des-Palmistes
Sainte-Rose
Saint-Leu
Pointe de Bretagne
Bras de la Plaine
Bras d'anjou
Riv. de l'Est
Pointe des Cascades
NATIONAL PARK
Piton de la Fournaise ▲ 2632m
Les Avirons
Entre-Deux
L'Étang-Salé
La Rivière
Le Tampon
Riv. d'lenmpfs
Saint-Louis
Bérive
Tremblet
Saint-Pierre
La Grète
Pointe de la Table
Petite-Île
Saint-Philippe
Saint-Joseph

Cirque de Mafate

Cirque de Mafate is a steeply-walled basin located in the north-west of Réunion. It was formed from the collapse of the large shield volcano, the Piton des Neiges. This very remote area was first settled in the 19th century by escaped slaves. It is entirely surrounded by mountains (photographed above). The cirque is owned by the government and managed by the Forestry Service. Today it is inhabited by small communities who are supported by the government. The largest village in the area is La Nouvelle (see inset).

not surprising, then, that Réunion is still heavily reliant on subsidies from France.

Natural resources are fish, arable land, and **hydropower**, and products include rum, maize, tobacco, and vanilla. Sugar cane was once by far the most important crop, but services are now predominant and tourism is encouraged.

OPPOSITE BELOW: The pristine beach of Grande Anse.

ABOVE: Bottlenose dolphins (*Tursiops truncatus*) forage in the crystal clear blue waters off Réunion in the Indian Ocean.

Text-Dependent Questions

1. Who is head of state in Réunion?

2. Who discovered Réunion?

3. What alcoholic drink is produced in Réunion?

RWANDA

R wanda has borders with the Democratic Republic of Congo, Burundi, Tanzania, and Uganda. It includes part of the beautiful Lake Kivu in the west, which has volcanic mountains to its north-east. Eastern Rwanda forms part of the Great Rift Valley and is bounded by the Kagera National Park and the Kagera river. The remainder of the country is rolling savanna grassland.

Words to Understand

Exiles: People in a situation where they are forced to leave their country and re-locate in another country.

Genocide: The deliberate killing of people who belong to a particular, political, cultural, or racial group.

Hunter-gatherer: A member of a culture who obtains food by hunting animals and gathering plants for food.

In the 10th century, Hutu people settled the area that was previously inhabited by Pygmy and Twa **hunter-gatherers**. In the 14th and 15th centuries the Hutu came under the domination of the immigrant cattle-owning Tutsi people, even though they were in the majority. The Tutsi established control throughout the land, almost as an aristocracy, and eventually founded a kingdom near Kigali. By the late 18th century, Ruanda and Burundi had united into a single Tutsi-dominated kingdom with a centralized military structure. The area was claimed by Germany in 1890, and was administered as part of German East Africa until 1918. It was occupied by Belgium forces during the First World War, eventually becoming part of the Belgian League of Nations mandate territory of Ruanda-Burundi.

Rwanda became independent as a republic in 1962, a few years after the Tutsi king had been violently overthrown by the majority Hutu people, and the Hutu Grégoire Kayibanda was made president.

OPPOSITE: Rwanda's capital city Kigali.

RIGHT: A family of mountain gorillas (*Gorilla beringei beringei*) in Volcanoes National Park that borders Virunga National Park in the Democratic Republic of Congo and Mgahinga Gorilla National Park in Uganda.

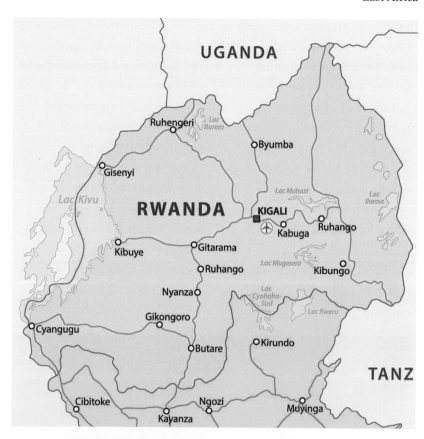

Over the next few years, thousands of Tutsi were killed and 200,000 were driven into exile in neighboring countries. Kayibanda was ousted in a military coup under General Juvénal Habyarimana in 1973, who became president five years later. Drought devastated Rwanda during the 1980s, followed by a period of inter-ethnic conflict after Tutsi exiles launched a raid in which many thousands were killed.

In 1990 the government was attacked by the Rwanda Patriotic Front (RPF), a Tutsi military-political organization, formed by the children of exiles and based in Uganda, when Habyarimana was forced to adopt a multi-party constitution. The period following was characterized by ethnic tensions and political and economic upheavals, which culminated in 1994 in the deaths of Habyarimana and the president of Burundi, who were assassinated when their aircraft was shot down, though it is uncertain who was responsible for the deed.

This triggered the Rwanda Genocide – a seemingly organized attempt to eliminate the Tutsi population. It ended in defeat for the Hutu regime, but not before more than 800,000 people, largely Tutsi and Hutu moderates, were slaughtered by predominantly Hutu supporters of the government.

Mount Sabyinyo

Mount Sabyinyo is an extinct volcano in eastern Africa in the Virunga Mountains. It is located north east of Lake Kivu, and west of Lake Bunyonyi in Uganda. The summit of the mountain, at 11,959 feet (3,645m), marks the intersection of the borders of the Democratic Republic of the Congo, Rwanda, and Uganda. It also lies within the adjoining national parks established by these countries: Virunga National Park in the DRC, the Volcanoes National Park in Rwanda, and Mgahinga Gorilla National Park in Uganda. The slopes of Mount Sabyinyo are a habitat for the mountain gorillas.

Fearing Tutsi retribution, over two million fled, including some responsible for the massacre, to Zaïre (the Democratic Republic of Congo) and neighboring countries. In 1997 Rwandan troops supported Laurent Kabila's successful overthrow of President Mobutu in Zaïre, but Kabila failed to expel Hutu militia from Congo. In 1996–97 Rwanda and Zaïre came to the brink of war after there were Tutsi killings of Hutu in Zaïre. A Hutu refugee crisis was averted as thousands were allowed to return to Rwanda.

In the first elections since the genocide, Paul Kagame of the RPF became president in 2002, with Bernard Makuza prime minister; both were re-elected in 2003. Paul Kagame remains president today.

A peace deal was made in 2002 with the Democratic Republic of Congo, in which Rwanda promised to withdraw its troops from the east

ABOVE: A tea plantation.

Text-Dependent Questions

1. In which century did the Hutu people first settle in the country?

2. Why did the genocide in Rwanda happen?

3. Why is Rwanda's economy struggling?

if Congo expelled the Hutu militias that had been hiding there since the early 1990s.

Fighting among ethnic groups, loosely associated political rebels, armed gangs, and various government forces in the Great Lakes region, overspilling into Burundi, DRC, Rwanda, and Uganda, have substantially moderated from a decade ago, due to UN peace-keeping, international mediation, and efforts by local governments to create civil societies. Nevertheless, 57,000 Rwandan refugees still reside in 21 African states, and 20,000 fled to Burundi in 2005 and 2006 to escape drought and

recriminations from traditional courts investigating the 1994 massacres. The 2005 DRC and Rwanda verification, designed to stem rebel actions on both sides of the border, remains in place

The most densely populated country in Africa, Rwanda has few natural resources and very little industry. Around 90 percent of the population is engaged in subsistence agriculture, which has trouble keeping pace with the growing population. The main exports are coffee, tea, pyrethrum, tin and hides, though exports are hampered by inadequate infrastructure.

The 1994 genocide decimated

Rwanda's already fragile economy, making the people far poorer than they already were; consequently, Rwanda has been receiving substantial foreign aid since then. The World Bank has praised Rwanda's recent development successes, which has helped to reduce poverty and inequality.

ABOVE: Zebras (*Equus quagga*) in Akagera National Park.

LEFT: Lake Kivu is one of the African Great Lakes. It lies on the border between Democratic Republic of Congo and Rwanda, and is in the Albertine Rift, the western branch of the East African Rift. Lake Kivu empties into the Ruzizi River, which flows southwards into Lake Tanganyika.

SEYCHELLES

An archipelago of 115 or so islands, located in the Indian Ocean to the north-east of Madagascar. Only 33 islands are inhabited; those around Mahé, where the capital Victoria is situated, and where most of the population is concentrated, are mostly granite, with a narrow coastal strip, and there are coral **atolls** elsewhere.

The islands are home to many **endemic** plant species, one of which – the coco-de-mer palm – has the

LEFT: Built in 1992, Arul Mihu Navasakthi Vinayagar Temple is the only Hindu temple in Seychelles.

BELOW: Waterside homes with boats moored in front of them, Eden, Mahé island.

OPPOSITE: A map of Seychelles.

largest seed of any plant. The Seychelles largely escaped the tsunami of 2004, though there was flooding and a loss of marine life and three people lost their lives.

The islands were explored by the Portuguese in the early 16th century. Colonized by the French from the mid-18th century, the Seychelles were seized by the British in 1794 and were made a dependency of Mauritius in 1810, becoming a separate crown colony in 1903.

Words to Understand

Atoll: A ring-shaped coral island.

Endemic: Common to a particular region or area.

Tsunami: A large, high wave in the ocean usually caused by an earthquake. On reaching land it can be destructive.

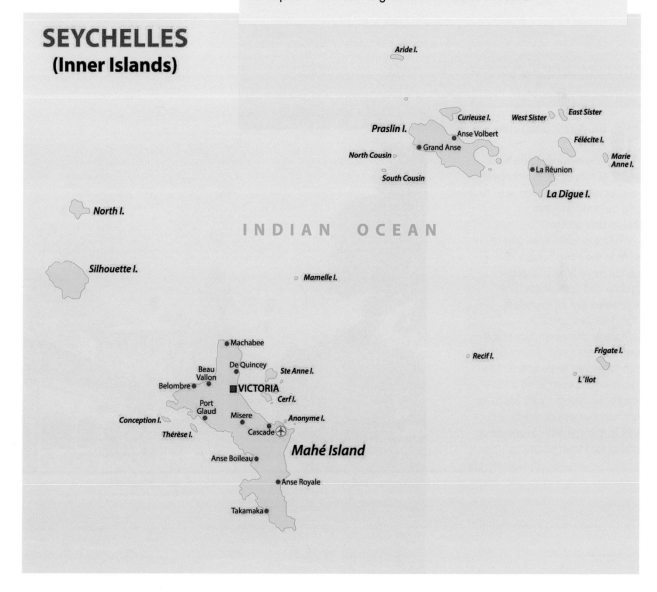

SEYCHELLES
(Inner Islands)

Aride I.

Curieuse I.   West Sister   East Sister

Praslin I.   Anse Volbert   Félécite I.

North Cousin   Grand Anse   Marie Anne I.

South Cousin   La Réunion

La Digue I.

North I.

INDIAN   OCEAN

Silhouette I.

Mamelle I.

Machabee   Recif I.   Frigate I.

De Quincey   Ste Anne I.   L'Ilot

Beau Vallon

Belombre   VICTORIA

Port Glaud   Cerf I.

Conception I.   Misere   Anonyme I.

Thérèse I.   Cascade

Anse Boileau   Mahé Island

Anse Royale

Takamaka

BELOW: The clock tower in Victoria resembles London's Big Ben.

OPPOSITE: Anse Cocos Beach on La Digue island.

OVERLEAF: The beautiful beach of Anse a La Mouche, on the island of Mahé.

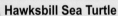

Hawksbill Sea Turtle

The hawksbill sea turtle (*Eretmochelys imbricata*) is a critically endangered sea turtle belonging to the Cheloniidae family.

While this turtle lives part of its life in the open ocean, it spends more time in shallow lagoons and coral reefs. The Seychelles are an important habitat for this species.

Several characteristics of the hawksbill sea turtle distinguish it from other sea turtle species. Its elongated, tapered head ends in a beak-like mouth (from which its common name is derived), and its beak is more sharply pronounced and hooked than others.

Independence as a republic within the Commonwealth was achieved in 1976, and the islands of Aldabra, Farquhar, and Des Roches, that had detached themselves in 1965 to form the British Indian Ocean Territory, were returned to Seychelles.

It was declared a one-party state in 1979, which lasted until 1992, the first free elections coming the following year. In 2001 France-Albert René was re-elected, having been president since the coup d'état in 1977. In 2004 he stepped down, and his vice-president, James Michel, took over the presidency; in July 2006 he was elected to a new five-year term and went on to win again in 2011.

Economic growth is led by the tourist industry, which provides 70 percent of revenue, though there have been recent moves to lessen dependency on tourism by developing light industries, farming, and tuna-fishing.

Text-Dependent Questions

1. What is the capital of Seychelles?

2. How many islands are inhabited in Seychelles?

3. What percentage of Seychelles's revenue is provided by tourism?

SOMALIA

A country that extends along the Gulf of Aden and the Indian Ocean, Somalia, previously known as the Somali Democratic Republic, occupies a strategic position on the Horn of Africa. It is bounded by Ethiopia and Djibouti to the west and north and by Kenya to the south-west. Predominantly dry grassland and semi-desert, the terrain is undulating in the north but flat in central and southern areas; irregular rainfall gives rise to recurrent, life-threatening drought. Arab traders began to migrate to the coastal areas from the 7th century, where they mingled with the indigenous Cushitic peoples; they also brought Sunni Islam with them, establishing Mogadishu as a center of trade and eventually as a sultanate in the 10th century.

The protectorate of British Somaliland was established in the north from 1884–87 and Italian Somaliland in the center and south from 1889. Italian Somaliland was established as a colony in 1927, and was incorporated into Italian East Africa in 1936. It was occupied by the British during the Second World War, who administered it until 1950, when it returned to Italian administration under UN trusteeship. Both became independent in 1960, the two joining together to form the United Republic of Somalia.

In 1969 the president was assassinated in a military coup, led by General Mohamed Siad Barre; the constitution was suspended, political parties were banned, and Siad Barre became president of a

Words to Understand

Constitution: A system of laws and regulations by which a country or state is governed.

Insurgents: People who fight or revolt against an established government.

Transitional government: A government temporarily set up to prepare the way for a permanent government.

ABOVE: Detail of the Laas Geel cave paintings near Hargeisa, Somaliland, depicting a cow.

OPPOSITE: A map of Somalia also showing the region of Somaliland.

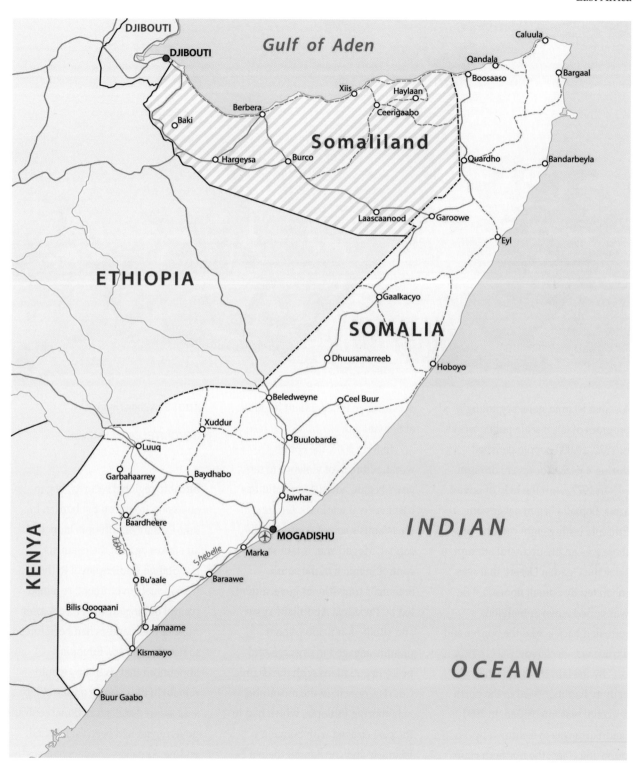

DJIBOUTI

DJIBOUTI

Gulf of Aden

Caluula

Qandala

Boosaaso

Bargaal

Xiis

Haylaan

Berbera

Ceerigaabo

Baki

Somaliland

Quardho

Bandarbeyla

Hargeysa

Burco

ETHIOPIA

Laascaanood

Garoowe

Eyl

Gaalkacyo

SOMALIA

Dhuusamarreeb

Hoboyo

Beledweyne

Ceel Buur

Xuddur

Buulobarde

Luuq

Garbahaarrey

Baydhabo

Jawhar

Juba

INDIAN

Baardheere

Shebelle

MOGADISHU

Marka

Bu'aale

Baraawe

KENYA

Bilis Qooqaani

Jamaame

Kismaayo

OCEAN

Buur Gaabo

socialist Islamic state, beginning a program of large-scale public works. In 1972, 20,000 people perished during a period of severe drought.

In 1977, with the help of Soviet arms, Somalia began a war with Ethiopia lasting eight months, when there was an unsuccessful attempt to seize the Ogaden Desert, that was inhabited by Somali nomads. The war ended when Somali forces retreated back across the border and a truce was declared.

By the late 1980s, guerrilla activity had increased in the north and civil war intensified. In 1991 Siad Barre was overthrown by opposing clans, the northern clans

declaring an independent Republic of Somaliland.

In May 2006, the country's worst outbreak of violence in ten years began, with Islamist militias battling rival warlords. On June 6, the Islamists seized control of the capital, Mogadishu, establishing control in much of the south. Somalia's **transitional government**, led by President Abdullahi Yusuf and situated in Baidoa, spent months engaged in unsuccessful peace negotiations with the Islamic Courts Council. In the meantime, neighboring Ethiopia, which had in the past clashed with Somalia's Islamists and considered them a

ABOVE: A camel market.

OPPOSITE: City of Hargeisa.

threat to regional security, began amassing troops on the border. In mid-December, Ethiopia launched air strikes against the Islamists.

Somali soldiers, loyal to the transitional government, regained control of Mogadishu. A week later most of the Islamists had been forced to flee the country. Ethiopia announced that its troops would remain in the country until stability was assured and a functional central government had been established, ending Somalia's 15 years of anarchy.

In January 2007, the US launched airstrikes on the retreating Islamists, believing they included three members of al-Qaeda suspected of involvement in the 1998 bombings of the American embassies in Nairobi and Dar es Salaam. These were strongly criticized in Muslim countries, which accused the Americans of killing Somali civilians.

Battles between the **insurgents** and Somali and Ethiopian troops intensified in March, leaving 300 civilians dead in what has been called the worst fighting in 15 years. It also created a humanitarian crisis, with more than 320,000 Somalis fleeing the fighting in Mogadishu in just two months. In July, a national reconciliation conference opened in

Mogadishu, but was quickly postponed when leading opposition figures failed to appear. The fighting intensified once again in October.

Since 2012, when a new internationally-backed government was installed, Somalia has been inching towards stability, but the new authorities still face a challenge from Al-Qaeda-aligned Al-Shabab insurgents.

A relatively new figure in

Somali politics, academic and civic activist Hassan Sheikh Mohamud beat the incumbent Sheikh Sharif Sheikh Ahmed in a run-off presidential vote in September 2012. This was the first presidential election held on Somali soil since 1967, and held among members of parliament elected by clan elders.

In February 2016 African Union leaders agreed on the need for more funding and support for their military presence after increased Al-Shabab attacks on public spaces and pro-government troops.

Somalia has relatively few resources and much of the economy has been devastated by civil war, deep political divisions, and natural disaster. In 2004 Somalia was one of the many countries devastated by the tsunami. Despite the lack of effective national governance, Somalia has maintained a healthy informal economy, largely based on livestock, remittance/money transfer companies, and telecommunications.

Text-Dependent Questions

1. Which three countries border Somalia?

2. What is Somalia's capital city?

3. What year was Somalia devastated by a tsumani?

TANZANIA

A republic formed by the union of Tanganyika and Zanzibar in 1964, Tanzania has a coastal plain that rises to a fertile plateau of savanna grassland, with the mass of Kilimanjaro to the north-east and the Livingstone Mountains to the south-west. It is bordered by Kenya, Uganda, Rwanda, Burundi, DR Congo, Zambia, Malawi, and Mozambique. It is bounded on the east by the Indian Ocean, and parts of Lakes Victoria, Tanganyika, and Nyasa (Lake Malawi) lie within its borders. Half the country is forested and it is home to wildlife parks of ecological importance, including the famous Serengeti National Park in the north.

Trading posts appeared along the coast, following the area's settlement by Omani Arabs in the 8th century. In 1499, Vasco da Gama visited the island of Zanzibar, and it was occupied by the Portuguese in the 16th century, together with the coastal states. In 1840, Sultan Seyyid bin Sultan moved his capital

BELOW: A family of elephants (*Loxodonta africana*) against the backdrop of Mount Kilimanjaro.

OPPOSITE: A map of Tanzania.

to Zanzibar and the trade in slaves and ivory flourished, though the sultanates of Zanzibar and Oman separated when the sultan died in 1861.

In the 19th century European explorers began to venture inland, followed by Christian missionaries. In 1884, in defiance of Zanzibar,

Words to Understand

Revolution: An attempt, usually a violent one, to end a government's rule and establish a new one.

Topography: The physical features in an area.

Trading block: An agreement between countries relating to reducing barriers for trade.

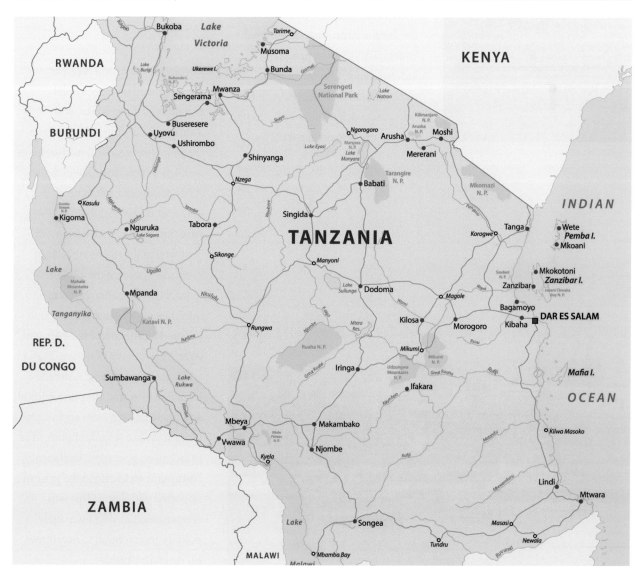

German colonization of the mainland began. In 1890 Zanzibar became a protectorate of Britain and German claims to the mainland were recognized. During the First World War, Tanganyika (part of German East Africa since 1897) was again taken by Britain and was held until 1946.

In 1954 Julius Nyerere organized the Tanganyikan African National Union (TANU) to campaign for independence, becoming prime minister in 1960. Independence from Britain was achieved in 1961, though the country remained part of the

LEFT: A Masai man in traditional red dress in the Serengeti National Park.

BELOW LEFT: Stone Town is the old part of Zanzibar City on the island of Zanzibar.

Commonwealth, and Nyerere became the first post-colonial president of Tanganyika, with Zanzibar achieving independence the following year. In 1964 there was a violent **revolution**, in which the Arab-dominated sultanate of Zanzibar was overthrown by the Afro-Shirazi Party, merging with Tanganyika the following year to eventually become the United Republic of Tanzania. Nyerere introduced African socialism, and initiated a program of self-help and equality by means of nationalization and collective farming. A decade later, however, and despite technical and financial help from abroad, the program was a singular failure, due to lack of co-operation, inefficiency, corruption and a rise in the price of imported petroleum. This was compounded in 1979 by a costly military intervention to overthrow Idi Amin in Uganda.

Ngorongoro Conservation Area

The Ngorongoro Conservation Area (UNESCO World Heritage Site) is located 110 miles (180km) west of Arusha in the Crater Highlands area of Tanzania. The area is named after Ngorongoro Crater, a large volcanic caldera within the area. It has a diverse wildlife population

The first multi-party elections were held in 1995, producing a comfortable win for Benjamin Mkapa. In 1999 Nyerere died and Tanzania withdrew from Africa's largest **trading block**. In 2000, President Mkapa, who had improved the economy over the preceding five years, was re-elected. The following year violence broke out between opposition supporters and troops on Zanzibar, after elections had been partially rerun, following allegations of irregularities. Tanzania's current president is John Magufuli who was elected in October 2015.

One of the poorest countries in the world, most of the population of Tanzania is rural and heavily dependent on agriculture: however, the system is primitive and **topography** and climate limit production. Nevertheless, Tanzania does receive technical and financial aid from abroad, and has been successful in attracting investment.

1. Which two countries united to form Tanzania in 1964?

2. What important national park is in the north of the country?

3. Who is Tanzania's current president?

UGANDA

Uganda is a **landlocked** republic, which has borders with Kenya to the east, Tanzania and Rwanda to the south and south-west, the Democratic Republic of Congo to the west, and Sudan to the north. The terrain consists of a savanna platform, rimmed by mountains and drained by the White Nile and Lakes Albert, Victoria, Kyoga, and Edward, all of which, apart from Kyoga, are shared with neighboring countries. Uganda is still predominantly agricultural and most of the people live in rural areas.

In the 16th century the Bunyoro kingdom was founded by

Words to Understand

Landlocked: A country or state surrounded by land.

Missionaries: People sent to foreign countries to convince others to join a religion and to help the sick and poor etc.

Paramilitary: An unofficial army that operates and is organized like an army.

immigrants from south-eastern Sudan. The 17th century saw the rise of the powerful Buganda kingdom in the south, from which Uganda gets its name. By the middle of the 19th century, Arab traders in ivory and slaves had reached Uganda, and

European explorers, such as Speke and Stanley, and the first Christian **missionaries**, had begun to arrive, leading to conflict with the pre-existing Muslim population. Uganda was placed under the charter of the British East Africa Company in 1888 and was ruled as a British protectorate from 1894, becoming independent within the Commonwealth in 1962.

The following year it was pronounced a federal republic with the Kubaka (King) Mutesa II of Buganda its head of state and Milton Obote of the Uganda People's Congress its prime minister. The king, who was opposed to a one-party state, was ousted in a coup by

LEFT: The hillside village of Jinja on the banks of the Victoria Nile.

OPPOSITE: Map of Uganda.

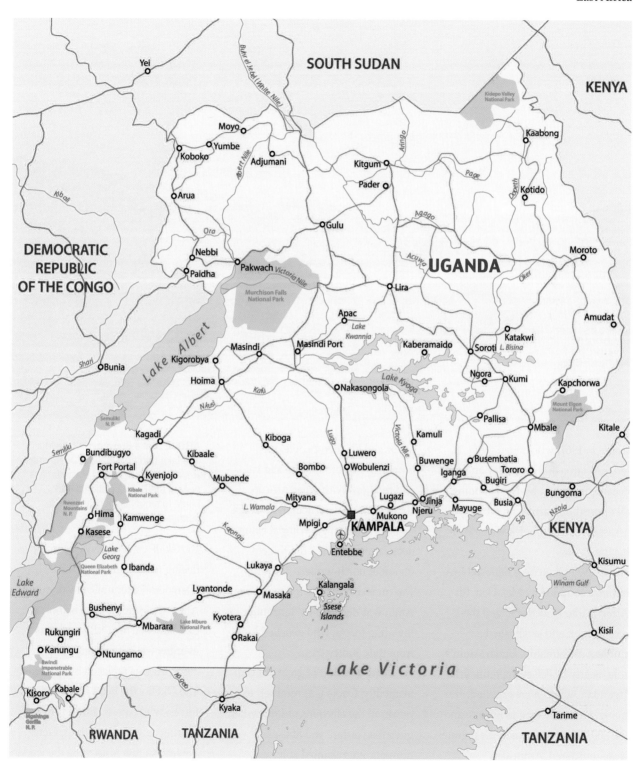

ABOVE: Lake Bunyonyi in Uganda. The lake borders Uganda, Democratic Republic of Congo, and Rwanda. It is near to the Bwindi National Park, home to mountain gorillas (*Gorilla beringei beringei*).

Obote in 1967, who ended the federal status of the country and became president himself, banning all opposition parties after an assassination attempt was made on his life in 1969.

In 1971 Obote was deposed in a military coup led by Maj.-Gen. Idi Amin Dada, who suspended the constitution and established a ruthless dictatorship. Under Amin's rule, nearly 50,000 entrepreuneurial Ugandan Asians were expelled, many of them fleeing to Britain, and the 300,000 who opposed the regime were murdered. Amin also terrorized his own people, the economy was brought to near ruin, and relations with other African states, Kenya in particular, to which Amin was making territorial claims, deteriorated. In 1978 the Kagera region of north-western Tanzania was annexed, but the following year Amin was defeated by Tanzanian invading forces, who expelled him from the country.

After a period of great political instability, Obote was returned to power in the elections of 1980, when guerrilla warfare and abuses of human rights claimed at least 100,000 lives, with twice as many fleeing to Rwanda and Zaïre (Democratic Republic of Congo). After opposition by the National Resistance Army (NRA), he was overthrown in a military coup in 1985 and was replaced by Brigadier Tito Okello, the head of the armed forces, who entered into a power-sharing agreement with Lt.-Gen. Yoweri Kaguta Museveni, the leader of the NRA. Museveni seized power the following year, headed a broad-based coalition government, and was re-elected in the first direct presidential elections in 1996. He then went on to win the 2001, 2006, 2011, and 2016 elections. Since becoming president, Museveni has improved human rights by cutting abuses perpetrated by the army and the police.

Since 1987, the cult-like Lord's Resistance Army (LRA), a **paramilitary** group operating mainly in northern Uganda, but which has overflowed into southern Sudan, has been conducting an armed rebellion against the government. The LRA is accused of violating human rights, which includes abductions, the use of child soldiers, and a number of massacres and mutilations. The aim of the LRA is to run the state according to its leader's eccentric interpretation of the Bible's Ten Commandments, but to further this cause, millions have been killed or kidnapped. The International Criminal Court issued arrest warrants on July 8 and September 27, 2005 against Joseph Kony, his deputy Vincent Otti, and other LRA commanders, three of whom died or were killed in the period July 2006 to mid-April 2008.

On August 4, 2006, after the Jubal peace talks, Otti declared a unilateral ceasefire and asked the Ugandan government to reciprocate. A truce was signed on August 26, 2006, under the terms of which, LRA forces would leave Uganda and gather in two assembly areas protected by the government of Sudan. On August 20, 2007, Uganda declared it was seeking legal advice on setting up a war crimes court. In November 2007, an LRA delegation journeyed to Kampala to restate their commitment to a peaceful resolution of the conflict before going on a tour of northern Uganda to meet victims of the insurgency and ask their forgiveness. Reports surfaced that Otti had been executed on or around October 8, 2007, following an internal power struggle. In July 2011 the US deployed special forces personnel to help Uganda combat LRA rebels. In 2012 the Ugandan army captured a senior LRA commander, Caesar Achellam in a clash in the Central African Republic. This was seen as a major breakthrough.

In 1993 the kubaka, in the person of Ronald Muwenda Mutebi II, was reinstated. In 1997, Uganda, along with other countries, became embroiled in the Democratic Republic of Congo's civil war, in an effort to depose President Mobutu, but DR Congo accused Uganda of maintaining its influence in DR Congo's mineral-rich east, while Uganda accused DR Congo of failing to disarm Ugandan rebels present in its territory.

Uganda has substantial natural resources, including fertile soil, adequate rainfall, and deposits of copper and cobalt. Agriculture is the most important sector of the economy, with coffee the principal export. Growth continues to be solid, despite the variability in the price of coffee. Economically, great strides have been made, but war, corruption, debt, failure to industrialize, and the slowness of the government to press home reforms, raise doubts as to Uganda's long-term prosperity.

Text-Dependent Questions

1. Who founded the Bunyoro kingdom?

2. When did Uganda gain independence?

3. Why is agriculture so successful in Uganda?

Index

PHOTOGRAPHIC ACKNOWLEDGEMENTS

All images in this book are supplied under license from © Shutterstock.com.

The content of this book was first published as *AFRICA*.

ABOUT THE AUTHOR
Annelise Hobbs

After completing her Classical studies, Annelise Hobbs became a librarian, working in a busy area of central London frequented by local authors and university students as well as the public itself. Eventually, she decided to use her extensive knowledge, and particularly her interest in travel, art, and architecture, to help in her research as an editor, inevitably progressing to writing books herself.

FIND OUT MORE:

Websites

- **Lonely Planet**
  www.lonelyplanet.com

- **Maps of Africa**
  www.worldatlas.com

- **National Geographic**
  travel.nationalgeographic.com

- **United Nations Educational, Scientific and Cultural Organization**
  http://whc.unesco.org

Further Reading by Mason Crest

AFRICA PROGRESS AND PROBLEMS
13 VOLUMES | 112 PAGES
Africa is a complex and diverse continent, and its more than 50 countries provide a study in contrasts: democracy and despotism, immense wealth and crushing poverty, modernism and traditionalism, peaceful communities and raging civil wars. The books in the AFRICA: PROGRESS AND PROBLEMS series take a close look at many of the major issues in Africa today, such as AIDS, poverty, government corruption, ethnic and religious tension, educational opportunities, and overcrowding. *2014 copyright*

THE EVOLUTION OF AFRICA'S MAJOR NATIONS
26 VOLUMES | 80 PAGES
Africa, with its rich natural resources and its incredible poverty, is a continent of contradictions. Each book in this series examines the historical and current situation of a particular African nation. Readers will learn about each country's history, geography, government, economy, cultures, and communities. *2013 copyright*